An Answer by God

Why God, why?

Ray Hope

First Published in **September 2024**

ISBN: 978-93-6356-153-3

PUBLISHING MONGERS

+91 9311101365

Distributed by: Watergies

Preface

The world is simple. It is us that have made it complicated. Imagine a world where everyone is good, no one is working to hurt you. That is the world God intended for us as humans. The only flaw with his plan was giving us free will. Free will to hurt others.

Foreword

The author provides a new perspective on life, religion and humanity. In the book, he asks a simple question and God comes to answer. It is an interesting read that explains whatever wrong happens, why does it happen and even if God sees that happening, why does he not intervene.

Acknowledgments

A heartfelt thanks to the publishing team and God for everything.

About the author

I am just a normal person living a normal life touched by God.

Dedication

This one is dedicated to God.

Introduction

An interesting encounter where you ask God a question and he answers. He changes your life while explaining whatever happens, has its reasons. He shows you the reasons and gives you the choice to play God. The end result is exactly what he expected, but he gives you the knowledge to take those decisions along the way and makes you a better person, makes you realise what really matters, because this is when he answered, this is An Answer By God.

Prologue

“

Contents

Chapter One
The Question

I am just a normal guy, with a normal life who has never encountered a miracle. I was not too religious either, I respected God, but never got into all of it. It was like if he exists, fine, you have my respect, but I have never met you so I will carry on with my life. But, who knew what was coming my way. It could be a dream, it could be real, I definitely can't be sure about it, but it felt real. It all started with just a simple question, "Why God, why ?" I had invested money into something, and it was a good deal that should have given me a good return, but out of the blue, it all went to hell and I asked out loud, "Why God, why ?" and then it all happened. I may have passed out, fainted or immediately slept, but I wasn't alone in my room anymore.

I woke up and there was this shining bright light that hurt my eyes for a moment, but I could see someone in my room. Now, my first instinct as would be anyone else's was to run for the baseball bat and hit the guy who broke into my home. But, as soon as I tried to pick up the bat, I could not lift it. It became too heavy to pick it up. I looked at the guy while still trying to pick up the bat, but he just stood there and smiled at me.

I ask, "Who are you ? What the hell are you doing in my room ?"

He replies, "You asked for me, and I am always listening. Sometimes, I answer personally."

I was confused and ask, "What are you even saying ? I am calling the cops. You should go before they get here."

He says, “Why don’t you try doing that ?”

I tried to pick up my phone, but that too became extremely heavy. I could not even pick up my phone.

I ask, “What did you do to my phone ?” I was still under the assumption that there was a stranger in my room, and was responding accordingly.

He asks, “Now, that you have done what you wanted to do, can we get to the matter at hand ?”

“I don’t even know what you are talking about.”

“You asked me a question personally. I am here to answer.”

“Please elaborate, I never asked anyone anything. I haven’t even talked to anyone since the morning.”

"You asked me by my name."

"I asked you what ? I don't even know your name, and why can't I pick up things ? What have you done to me ? Did you drug me ?"

He smiles and replies, "You asked why God, why and here I am to answer. I have done nothing to you. You are not in your body right now, you are just a soul. Your body could not have survived talking to me in this form, and I did not drug you."

I just stare at him blankly, trying to process what he just said. God, with a capital G, no way God looks like an average human. I am being scammed, that is for sure, and I probably have been drugged too. Let's see what they want, I just need to not give them my banking password, no matter how compelling they are.

He says, “I don’t want your banking password.”

I never said that out loud, how did he know what I was thinking ? Maybe with the drugs, I am thinking out loud and don’t realise that.

He says, “All your doubts will be answered for soon.”

I decided to go with the flow now, and figure out what he wants. I say, “You came to answer a question, I am waiting. Give me the answer.

“For you to understand the answer, you need the knowledge.”

I say, “Enlighten me.”

“Enlightenment is not what you can achieve in a day. It takes lifetimes.”

I sigh and say, “I did not mean that literally. Impart the knowledge or whatever you have in mind.”

He says, "I cannot tell you anything. Whatever I say, you are not going to believe a single word of it. You will have to see for yourself."

"Alright, I will play your game. If you are God, why is there misery ? Why do people starve to death ? Why do people die untimely ? Why do people beat each other ? Why do people get hurt ? Why do people get their hearts broken ? Why is there rape ? Why is there crime ? Let's go full philosophical. Answer it, or show me, whatever."

"So many things happen at every second, and everything is accounted for."

"I thought you were going to show me something."

"Let's go, try on my shoes, and you will have your answers."

Suddenly that eye-hurting white light appears again, and we are somewhere else. There are people around. But, they do not care that we just appeared out of thin air.

He says, “They cannot see us.”

I ask, “Why are we here ?”

“For you to learn.”

Chapter Two
The Beggar

I look around, and we are in a street. There are lots of people coming and going. I see a beggar in the corner, a street vendor selling hotdogs, some shops where people are coming in and going. Nothing out of the ordinary.

I ask, “What am I looking for ?”

He says, “You asked about misery. Who is the most miserable person you see around here ?”

I take another look around, and I will have to go for the beggar. I say, “That guy, the one sitting in the corner. He has got to be the one.”

He replies, “Let’s go with him if you want. Everyone you see has their story, but let’s go with the one you find the most miserable. The beggar. Let’s just look at him for a moment and see how miserable he is.”

“That is bad. You are a sadist. Why would you want to look at a guy down on his luck. You can make him the richest guy with the snap of a finger, but you want to look at him in pain. What kind of a God are you ?”

A woman comes in front of him, and at the corner, she throws her garbage without caring about the guy. There was a little garbage there before, but how can a sane human throw trash alongside another person. I wanted to go and help the guy, but apparently I cannot be seen and I cannot touch anything.

I say, “Help the guy out, this is inhuman.”

He says, “Maybe, but you have to know his story.”

“No matter what his story his, nobody deserves this.”

“I give you the option to make him the richest guy on the planet at the end of this. You will have to decide that.”

“Alright”

“Let’s go somewhere else.”

The white light returns and we are in a house, it is not of someone who is rich, but it is somewhat tasteful. I take a look around, and find nothing out of the ordinary. A little girl playing in her room, she might be just two years old. She looks happy, playing around with her dolls. While jumping with the doll on various things, she drops a bowl. It shatters into pieces, and a man comes in her room. He is well dressed, but it looks like I know him from somewhere. I just can't put my finger on it. He slaps the girl, and shouts at her. Scolding a child is alright I suppose, that is how they will learn, but slapping her and screaming at her was a little uncalled for. He locks her in her room and goes out.

I say, "Not cool, but he is the parent. What can we do here ?"

He replies, "We can follow him."

He gets into his car, and drives away. We are like flying behind him. We are not up in the air, but we are pulled by the car.

I ask, “This ride is fun, but where are we going ?”

He replies, “Wherever he goes.”

We stop at a bar, and he starts ordering drinks. He meets a few people and looks like he is well known among them. He has a lot of drinks, and I could myself use one right now with everything that is going on. After what feels like forever watching him get drunk, he gets up and walks to his car. He can barely walk straight, but gets in and drives. We fly behind him again, and he jumps a traffic signal. A car coming in at the intersection tries to navigate him, but bangs into a pole. Even they were overspeed, and they did not even look at the car in front until the last second. The car is thrashed, there is no way anyone inside survived. He stops his car, gets out, takes a look and drives away.

I say, “He did not even call an ambulance. He could have made an anonymous call.”

He says, “The cameras have him on video jumping the signal and causing the accident.”

“I agree, but he could have saved a life maybe. It was unlikely, but there was still a chance.”

We start flying behind him again, and I say, “He is going the wrong way. He is skipping town. What about the little girl he locked up in her room ?”

He replies, “Let’s go and see.”

It looks like the girl has been here for a while. She is miserable. There are no windows in her room, and a two year old cannot break through a door. We look at her for what feels like an eternity, and she passes out.

I say, “Help her.”

He says, “No one can help her. Her father abandoned her and skipped town. This was how long she had to live. She has left this world.”

I say, “But you are God. Do something.”

“We will come back here.”

Chapter Three
The Beaten Wife

The white light returns and we are in another house. I still could not get over watching a little girl starving to death. I look around, and I see two kids now.

I say, "Don't kill them too. Why would you kill children ?"

He does not say a word, and soon, a woman walks inside the house. The kids go and hug her.

I say, “That is the mother, but wait a minute. She is the one who threw the garbage at the beggar.”

“Correct”

“Well, she has two personalities. She looked like a bitch before, but here she is nurturing. The kids do love her.”

“They do.”

She cooks up a meal for the kids, and then helps them study. She even plays with them and puts them to sleep. She looked like a perfect mother doing everything right.

After putting the children to sleep, as she walks out of their room, the door opens again and walks in her husband. Like a devoted wife, she puts the food on the table and the husband out of nowhere grabs her hand, and slaps her. He continues to slap her for a few minutes barking out random things in his life. What he had been through the day, and what his life is. He probably had a stressful day and he took it out on his wife. He keeps beating her, lifts up her dress and fucks her while she is still crying from the beating. After he is done, he pushes her on the table and walks away.

I ask, “Why do you let people be like this ?”

He replies, “Everyone usually is made the same. Two legs, two hands, a face, ten fingers, ten toes and everything. What they do with that, that is their choice. I do not control them. It is their free will.”

The husband leaves the house and is taking a walk to get somewhere.

There is no impact on his face of how he tortured and beat his devoted wife, a mother that loves his children and takes care of them while he just walks in, eats the food she prepared, beats her, rapes her and walks away.

He walks for a few minutes, and in front of an alley, a man in a black mask walks in front of him and points the knife at him. The guy who was the lion a few minutes back in his house is now a mouse. He is trying to protect his belongings, but the mugger punches him to the ground. He just lies down in the dirt, weeps and hands over his wallet.

I ask, “So you justify mugging of a wife beater ?”

“It will be for you to decide. Let’s go.”

Chapter Four
The Mugger

There was that white light again, and we saw the mugger hiding, removing the mask, keeping it in his pocket. Then he opened up the wallet, took all the cash out and tossed the wallet in the bin. We flew behind him, and he went to a departmental store and bought some food.

I ask, "Was he hungry ?"

He replies, "Let's find out."

"I don't know, whatever it was, whoever he mugged, I cannot justify mugging."

"That will be for you to decide."

We follow him into his home, and again, there is a completely changed personality. His home is not broken up per se, but it looks like he actually has no money. He opens up the food, calls out his kid and puts that food on the table. Our wife beater did not have enough money in his wallet to let him buy food for the both of them. He decides to stay hungry, but there is a smile on his face because he can feed his kid.

I say, "Maybe I believe in his cause, but not the means to achieve it."

The doorbell rings, and he opens up the door. An elderly woman and a young man walk in. The woman wishes him happy birthday, and gives him a gift. The man casually wishes him too. Apparently, they are his mother and brother. He offers them water while thanking them, but the brother taunts him on every occasion he gets. The mother dismisses those taunts, but the brother leaves no opportunity. He criticises him for wasting money on his education, getting a degree, and not be able to get a job. The brother is well to do, but he is involved in drugs. He even points out that dealing drugs is much better than wasting a life on education. After the mother intervenes, the brother starts brutally insulting him.

I say, "That was uncalled for. Forcing a guy into drugs, when he is constantly refusing. I guess mugging trumps drugs after all."

He says, "I guess so."

The brother gets all heated up when he is repeatedly refused the offer of dealing drugs. He pushes him away and calls him useless and a burden. He decides to not stay anymore in that dump and walks out.

I ask, "Now, I really feel for our mugger. Being forced into drugs, down on his luck, and a child to feed. I guess it was a good thing that he mugged that wife beater rapist."

He says, "That is again for you to decide. Let's go with him."

Chapter Five
The Dealer

The white light returns, and we follow the brother who gets in his car and goes to pick up his girlfriend. They drive to a club and meet a few more friends.

I say, "Looks like the drug dealer has his life figured out."

He says, "Maybe he does, maybe he does not."

The brother and his girlfriend have expensive drinks, order food, dance, laugh and continue drinking. They really seemed happy with their lives. I mean dealing drugs really pays. Bottle after bottle followed by those lights and cheers come to their table and they have a blast with it.

The girl walks away from the table. I assumed she was going to the restroom as did the others at the table. I was a little uncomfortable when we were following her there. She reached the restroom, and walked past it. She got to a corner and started making out with another one of their friends.

I say, "Oh, come on. If you are going to cheat, why do it with your boyfriend with you. Do it separately. Go get drunk on your own money. At least, have that courtesy. This is not cool."

He shrugs and says, "Free will."

The girl must have been drunk or maybe careless, but she spent quite some time there and the brother now seemed to worry. He comes looking for her, and after checking everywhere, finally reaches the corner. That is where they used to make out, so it did not take him long to find it. He is shocked, insulted and embarrassed to see his girlfriend with his friend. He lashes out with anger and pulls the guy off. Apparently, word gets around and the guy had more friends and acquaintances in the club. They beat the brother badly leaving him bleeding and broken down. The girl bends down with a smile on her face and says that they are done. She is breaking up with him.

I say, "Bitch, I am sorry. I did not mean that."

He laughs and says, "She really is a bit though."

After leaving the brother there, the girl and the guys that beat him walk out of there, leaving him there to take care of the bill. The guy kisses the girl again and leaves with his friends. Since the girl came with the brother, she decides to walk home.

I ask, "No consequences for them ? They just beat a guy in a public place after making out with his girlfriend, and what about the girl ? She really did a number on him."

He replies, "Let's find out."

Chapter Six
The Cheater

The white light appears again, and we join the girl walking down the street. The girl is least bothered with what just happened and texts her friends about how cool her night was.

I say, "This is what is wrong with society."

A car comes from back, and slows down besides her. It is the acquaintances of the guy that she was with. They helped her beatdown her boyfriend.

She knows that they are not here for anything good, and decides to ignore them and keep walking. The guys call her out for a minute, but since she kept ignoring them, stop the car in front of her, and pull her in. She screams, but her date is lying down in his own blood at the club. There is no one around to save her.

The guys take turn going at her, and she is helpless. She tries to fight, but she is no match for four guys. She finally gives up and bears with it, disgusted at what is happening to her and regrets cheating on her boyfriend and ending things.

I say, “There is no one around to help her. No matter how much I hate her, no one deserves this.”

I get no reply. She just lies still once they are done with her. They pick her up and throw her out.

I say, “Are you not going to do anything ? You punished the girl for what she did to her boyfriend, but what about those guys ? The guys that beat up an innocent guy, left him for dead and then betrayed their friend and raped his girl. Where is your justice ? Where is your karma ?”

He smiles and says, “Watch out.”

Chapter Seven
The Friends

I was expecting a white light again, and going to another place to see what happens, but the light does not appear. The guys just drive on, and stop at the traffic signal. Once it turns green, they shout goodbye to the girl and drive fast to escape the scene.

From the other side on the intersection, a car jumps its traffic signal and the guys navigate to save the crash, but instead bang into a pole. I am shocked to see the person getting out of the car. It is the same guy that left his daughter to starve and die.

I say, "No. This can't be."

He says, "You are not seeing things in the same order you believe them to be."

"But .."

He interrupts me and says, "Let's see where he goes."

I say, "But we already did. He is going to skip town and let his daughter starve to death. I don't want to see that again."

"I am not saying we are going to the house, let's see what happens to him."

We follow the car, flying behind him all the way two towns over. In the way, he gets out and throws away his phone. Then he ditches his car. Then after staying low for a day, he takes a bus to get back to his daughter. He goes to his house and finds police taking the body of her child. They found his daughter dead when they came in looking for him. They are looking everywhere for him and he has no way to go. Every friend he has ever known, the police are watching them. He has no car anymore. His bank accounts have been seized. All the things he ever owned are now with the police. He has no choice but to just walk from there. He walks around for a few hours, and then goes sit down in a corner.

I say, "No, I knew I had seen him before. It is the beggar. The one that was starving. He is even wearing the same clothes. That is how he ended up here. I cannot believe it."

He says, "Now, it is upto you whether you want to make him the richest person on the planet."

Chapter Eight
The Answer

I did not say a word. I frankly did not know what to say. From what he showed me, everyone is bad.

He says, “Now, let me show you something else.”

The white light appeared again, and we are in another home. I saw a guy sitting on a laptop, saying please God, please. Well, I was saying why God why, so I develop a soft corner for him. He looks at the screen for about thirty minutes, and jumps in celebration.

I ask, “What happened ?”

He replies, “He made some money.”

“Alright, but why are we here ? Is he going to use that money to destroy someone’s life and he is going to pay it some other way ?”

“No, it ends with this.”

“I am confused. No mugging, no rapes, no beating up, no accidents, nothing ?”

“Yes”

“Please elaborate.”

"This is the guy that was betting against you in that trade. Whatever you lost, he made it."

I immediately lost my soft corner for him, and say, "But why ? What did I ever do to him ? I don't even know him. Did I unintentionally hurt him in any way ?"

"No"

"Then why does he get to win from me ?"

"Let's see."

He goes out to the living room where his ten year old son just came from school. He says that he got a letter from school. If he does not deposit the fees within two days, they will not let him enter the premises. He smiles and says that he has the fees, and his child does not need to worry anymore. He will always be there for him, and he thanks God for letting him provide for his child.

I say, "Alright, I feel it for him. He needed it, he should have it. But why did he need it from me ?"

He replies, "You have enough. What you lost, it does not matter to you. What he won, that changes his life. If he had lost today, he would have been done. He would have lost all hope and he would have never been able to make an investment again. What you lost today, it will make you sad for a few minutes, but you will be making another investment tomorrow, and you will earn ten times of what you lost today. That tenfold return will make you much happier than you are sad today. But, what you lost today, that changed that man's life."

"I see your point. I don't agree with the means, but here, the end justifies the means."

"Let's go."

The white light comes in again, and we come back into my house.

He says, "You asked me 'God, why is there misery ? Why do people starve to death ? Why do people die untimely ? Why do people beat each other ? Why do people get hurt ? Why do people get their heart's broken ? Why is there rape ? Why is there crime ?' You saw the beggar miserable, you know why he deserved that and how he got there. You saw the little girl starving to death and the mugger's hungry child. You know how that happened. You saw the rapists dying an untimely death. You saw that happen with your own eyes twice. You asked about people beating each other. You saw the wife beater and the brother of the mugger. You asked about crime, you saw the mugging and why he did it. You asked about broken hearts, you saw the brother of the mugger in the club getting his heart broken and beaten up after that. You asked about rape, you saw what happened to his girlfriend. Most of all, you asked why, God why. You saw that the father needed the money more than you needed it today. This was just your question in one specific cycle. Billions of people are daily doing something, that goes in their Karmic accounts. They get their result accordingly and automatically. Some might get them immediately, some might take a while, some might even take a lifetime. But, they all answer for their deeds, for all their sins. I believe you have the knowledge now."

"I guess I do."

"What you do with it is upto you. I am always listening. I am omnipresent, but I cannot be answering all calls personally. I listen, I help wherever there is a need or a possibility to intervene. But, human beings have to decide their course on their own."

"So, if I have never done a bad deed, nothing bad is going to ever come my way ?"

"Are you sure you have never done a bad deed ?"

"Not intentionally."

"Think again."

I think for a second, and he continues, "Whatever options just came to your mind, they stand in your account, and you will get the result accordingly. Not only this, the deeds that you did in past lifetimes, they too are standing there, waiting to be settled."

"Past lifetime deeds should be settled in those lives. How can you punish someone for something that they have never known they did."

"Why do you think that a child is born in a palace as a king, and another on the street, to a beggar. The king has a luxurious life ahead, but the beggar has a miserable life ahead. How do you think that is decided ?"

"I always believed it to be a random order. I always thought that there was a line of souls, a waiting period and everyone goes into the next available kid as per their order in the cue."

He chuckles and says, "No. The karmic account follows you and you get allotted accordingly. A king can be cruel or kind, that adds to his account and he is placed accordingly in his next birth."

"Alright, why are there riots over religion then ? All of them think they have got that one true God. Do you support a particular group ?"

"There is only me. People see me in their own images. They might call me Jesus, Shiva, Allah, Ram, Nanak, whatever they like. But, it was always me. They made me in their own images and started fighting in my name. Human beings choose their own course. I am not the one to intervene."

"Why did that little girl die ? I mean she could have committed no sins in this lifetime."

"She did not, but she had in her last life. She came here to wash them off, and she did. Now, her next life will be good. She has already taken birth. She is born in Italy in a loving home where she is always going to be treated like a queen."

"I guess that makes sense. But, why can't everyone be equal. Give us a look into the account. Let us now how red we are in, and let us work towards going in the green."

"If humans got their hand on it, they are going to convert it into a currency. Imagine someone robbing a helpless person of all his good deeds. This way, even if you are in the positive, a good person will keep accumulating more points by doing a good deed every chance they get. Whereas, a person who has committed some sins along the way, will devote all their time to wash them off."

I ask, "Is there any chance to free ourselves of our sins ? Past lives and present ones too."

He chuckles again and says, "Ask for my forgiveness. Maybe I erase your account if I feel satisfied."

“Why don’t you give everyone a fresh start, and let them know that. No one will do a bad deed then.”

“And break the system ? How will someone be born ? Where would be the reward for being good all those past lives ? Where would be the punishment for all your sins ? Where would be the justice for all those people you hurt ?”

“Fine, but why me ? Why did you tell me all this ? What did I do to deserve this ? I am glad you chose me, but what made me special ?”

“You asked why God, why and I came. There was nothing special. I just came because you called. I sometimes do that. Moreover, you will know it was me. You will know my presence. But, if you tell anyone about this, they are going to laugh you out, maybe even call you mad.”

“So, you came to mess around with me ?”

“No, I came to impart knowledge. You have it now, it will be your choice what you do with it. You said ‘enlighten me’. You can work towards that, or you can work towards good deeds. Good deeds cancel out the bad ones. The choice will be yours.”

“Hey, on a side not, can you like clear my account of all the bad points all through eternity ?”

“Keep asking, keep praying, maybe someday I will.”

“Okay, that is diabolical, but it suits you, and frankly makes sense.”

“One last thing, I gave you the choice to make that beggar the richest man on the planet. Do you want to do that ?”

"No. No way, not after all he did."

"Now you know it all. You accounted his deeds and you decided. You have the knowledge, and your answer. My work here is done. See you in another lifetime."

Before I could even say goodbye or thank you, the white light filled the room again, and I woke up on my desk, looking at the money I lost. I still don't know if that was a dream or not, but the next day, my trades skyrocketed and I made ten times of what I lost.

After that day, I lost the want for anything materialistic. I am not saying I don't like them anymore, but I don't long for it. My focus has been on living my life without hurting anyone, and impart this knowledge on anyone I can find. I have impacted the lives of over a million people. They call me their spiritual leader, but I am not one, I am nobody. I am not a religion. I am just a normal guy living a normal life with the only goal of making another person's life a better place. Do no bad and the world will be a beautiful place. In the end, all I can say is -

'It could be a dream, it could be real, I definitely can't be sure about it, but it felt real.'

Epilogue

I give a speech as hundred of people gather to listen what I have to say. I say, "There is only one God, one true God, who you believe him to be. All he cares about his what we do, we do good or bad. For him, nothing else matters. I am not a prophet, I am someone just like you, but he chose me. I cannot tell you how, but this is his message .."

www.ingramcontent.com/pod-product-compliance
Lightning Source LLC
LaVergne TN
LVHW050340160826
845677LV00014B/3716

* 9 7 8 9 3 6 3 5 6 1 5 3 3 *